To John & Edith -

Nothing but Pleasant memories

Bill & Marie Kenney

The Beauty of
RENFREW
and AREA

ONTARIO CANADA

PAT & ROSEMARIE KEOUGH

A NAHANNI PRODUCTION

Copyright ©Patrick and Rosemarie Keough

Published by Nahanni Productions Inc., 400 Meyer Road, Salt Spring Island, British Columbia, Canada V8K 1X4. Fax 001-250-653-4994.

Canadian Cataloguing in Publication Data

Keough, Pat, 1945 -
       The Beauty of Renfrew and Area

ISBN 0-9692557-4-8

1. Renfrew (Ont.) — Pictorial works.
I. Keough, Rosemarie, 1959 -
II. Title

FC3099.R45K46 1998   979'.997138104'0922   C93-09179-7
F1059.5.R46K46 1998

Printed and bound in Canada.

Photographic Notes

Film: Kodachrome 25 and 200, and Ektachrome 64X, 100S, 100SW, and 200.
Cameras: 35mm Nikon FM2 and Nikon F5, with an assortment of Nikkor lenses.

Dedication

To Mom and Dad, Mary and Gerald Keough, with our love and appreciation. Over the many years and through all our adventures, near and far, you have always been there for us with your love, prayers, and support.

This book is also dedicated to Renfrew's other wonderful senior citizens, as well as the volunteers and staff of the RENFREW AND AREA SENIORS' HOME SUPPORT. You continue to help build the solid foundation of this community and set the path for young feet to follow.

Cousins Heather and Erin Mulvihill at Ma-te-way Park for the June 1993 Renfrew Girl's Softball League home opener, Calabogie versus Renfrew.

While cattle peacefully graze, heedless of the noise, the barns on Hugh Sholea's farm are blurred by the exhaust plumes from three thundering diesel electric engines, with a combined 9,800 horsepower, pulling a hundred-car, westbound freight into Renfrew on the Chalk River subdivision of the C.P.R. line.

At right in the heart of Renfrew, Raglan Street, the main thoroughfare, runs from top to bottom flanked by Plaunt and Argyle streets. The Canadian Pacific Railway cuts a diagonal line across town. In 1872 the first trains came to Renfrew along these tracks, then the Canada Central Railway.

This book, published on the eve of the new millennium, is a celebration of Renfrew and its surrounding area. Without a doubt, Renfrew is the epitome of all that is good and appealing about small-town Ontario. Renfrew continues to maintain a strong identity while adapting to the many pressures of the modern world. The town has direction. It knows where it is going, what it is, and, with equal importance, from where it came.

Roughly 180 years ago, a short time relatively speaking, a drifter named Coyle and Joseph Brunette, a lumber jobber, hacked out the first clearings for their shanties in the dense, deciduous forest along the Bonnechere River near Second Chute. The abundance of timber, land, and water power attracted other men, who soon followed with their families. These people lent their energy and ingenuity to the fledgling settlement, building the foundations of the fine community we see today. Their names echo down through the years: Henry Airth, Francis Xavier Plaunt, John Smith, Sampson Coumbs, William Logan, John Lorn McDougall, Francis Hincks, J. A. Jamieson, Martin Russell, A. A. Wright, Tom Low, and M. J. O'Brien, to mention a few. Their contributions, among others, are remembered, respected, and well documented in numerous local history books.

While photographing this area from time to time over the past 30 years, we endeavoured to capture the essence of what makes the region so special for us. Not surprisingly, given the interval, some of our photos are themselves now of a historic nature. Included among the following images are several of people who are now deceased, buildings that have been altered or demolished, and landscapes that have changed. In spite of the passage of time, what has remained constant is the friendly warmth of the people, the rural tranquility of the farms, and the scenic beauty of the region, with its lakes, streams, and forested hills.

We took most of our photographs when composition and light combined in a way that appealed to our sense of the aesthetic. Our objective was to record beautiful moments: when ice and hoarfrost lent a fleeting magic to a view of the Bonnechere River and the historic grist mill; or when the last warm rays of the sun touched the kindly faces of a man and his wife standing together on their porch. With artistic merit being our principal guiding factor, we have not included pictures of every church, school, or subdivision, the industrial park, or the hospital. The photos we share in this book are among those we consider our favourites.

We found the process of selecting the images from years of material to be a nostalgic task. So many good memories were rekindled while looking at familiar places and faces. This was especially so for Pat, Renfew having been his home town and the place he was raised and had his first adventures.

For a young boy, the long, lazy summer days were spent rambling through the fields and woods or playing in the hayloft of an old barn. There were swimming excursions to Hurd's Lake and up-country to Lake Clear. Smith's Creek, flowing sinuously beneath a canopy of willows, was a paradise to be explored by young pirates on rickety rafts. All winter long, children played hockey and games of chase on the frozen creek. Everyone learned to ski at the Pinnacle hill, with its old, frayed rope-tow. Later, the new and bigger slopes at Dacre and then Calabogie beckoned. After a day of skiing or ice-fishing, frequently there was the pleasure of hot chocolate and a chat beside the glowing pot-bellied stove in the likes of Frank Legris' or Pat Lynch's general stores.

There was the challenge of sneaking undetected beneath the fairgrounds' fence at the Fall Fair, and then sneaking back out again with enough empty pop bottles to earn change to buy tickets for rides. Afterward, who could resist the thrill of watching five, great, puffing and billowing steam locomotives struggle to pull the lengthy carnival train up the long C.N.R. grade out of town.

For a venturesome youth, there was the great fun of running an old, pump hand-car along the all-but-deserted, weed-covered K.&P. line, or climbing a hundred feet up the fire tower at Mount St. Patrick. On the Ottawa River near Castleford there were extensive log booms to run along or be pushed from.

Then, as now, everyone knew everyone else — and just about everything about everyone else's business, private or otherwise. People were friendly and, for the most part, helped one another. Sure there were feuds and spats, and the odd black eye, but nothing was ever too serious and all was soon forgotten.

The stillness of the night was frequently broken by the mournful whistle of a passing train. This sound, and a steady diet of *National Geographic* magazines, never failed to conjure up dreams of travel that eventually lured Pat away from home to a lifetime of exciting experiences in far corners of the world.

Returning for family visits, we both find that not too much has changed. Certainly Renfrew is a little bigger, with a fancy, new recreation complex and a few additional subdivisions, streets, and factories, as well as the mall at the edge of town. However, the train whistle still calls throughout the night, though all but the C.P.R. tracks have been torn up. The abandoned right-of-ways are well enjoyed by walkers, bicyclists, and ski-dooers. In spite of the changes, Renfrew has maintained its distinction, charm, and a lot of its appealing, laid-back ambience.

In some ways Renfrew is similar to the hub of a wheel. Town folk head out in every direction on weekends and holidays to enjoy cottages, hunt-camps, bush lots, and the countryside. Those who live in the neighbouring townships on the farms and in the outlying villages come into Renfrew for supplies, services, and other necessities, as well as for events such as the Remembrance Day ceremonies, Santa Claus Parade, Winter Carnival, Lumber Baron Days, Fall Fair, and the nearby Valley Bluegrass Festival.

The very existence of these and other festivities that occur throughout the year attests to the community spirit shared by the people of Renfrew and area. Unfortunately, this spirit is no longer so evident in a great number of other small towns scattered across the province. Many have lost much of their character and vitality as they are swallowed up and become bedroom communities for nearby burgeoning cities. The new residents of these absorbed towns often lack roots and a sense of belonging. Frequently faced with a long, tiring commute, these people have little time, energy, or inclination to participate in their community. The parades and festivals have all but come to an end. The music has stopped. Not so in Renfrew! By the grace of its fortuitous location and the strength of character of its citizens, Renfrew continues to be a dynamic community.

People in the town and in the surrounding countryside have an obvious keen interest and pride in their area. Perhaps this is why such a great wealth of informative local history books has been written over the last 100 years. We hope, in turn, that our simple book, with its many colour photographs, will add a new dimension to the body of work already in print. We wish to convey, through our images, a sense of this special place as it appears today, at the close of the 20th century.

As evening approaches, Nick and Doris Van Leyen and their dog, Lassie, enjoy the sun's last warm rays from their porch at 417 Raglan Street North. The many white hydrangeas and red geraniums are but part of the beautiful gardens surrounding their home, testimony to the couple's green thumbs.

The rising sun will soon melt the frost dusting the meadow grass. In 1992 Peter Barr's cross Hereford/Simmental herd moves toward the hollow below the rail fence where Smith's Creek flows out of sight. Beyond, the homes of Horton Heights stand on the rise that was once the Greg Kedrosky farm.

Upper Left and Right: The colourful 1998 Lumber Baron Parade, part of an annual four-day festival, proceeds along central Raglan Street.

Lower: Southwest of town along the Opeongo Line, we noticed the simple beauty of a weathered fence sagging through a field dappled with chicory.

This phantom, Ruth Elliot, certainly knows how to celebrate Halloween and welcome young trick-or-treaters. Getting right into the spirit of the season, Ruth adorns her 15 Harry Street home with a "spooky" flair, complete with ghosts, goblins, pumpkins, squash, corn stalks, and autumn foliage.

A repetition of pattern in the sprinkler's spray and in the fronds of potted plants adds extra interest to this gracious home at 560 Raglan Street South. Built in 1916 for lumber baron Allan Francis, the house harmoniously blends Georgian features with columns topped by Doric and Corinthian capitals.

Snow at Christmas time enhances the warm, inviting beauty of the Renfrew Presbyterian Church and manse. Pastor Martin Kreplin enters the main sanctuary, a remarkable stone edifice built in 1925. The manse, of complementary style, was added 25 years later using similar dressed limestone.

In the modern steeple of St. Francis Xavier Catholic Church hangs the one-ton bell blessed in 1882 and salvaged from the ruinous church fire of 1964.

In 1899 the present St. Andrew's United Church was built on the high ridge above the Madawaska River in Burnstown, today a charming village.

In mid-July on the farm of Gord and Laurie MacMillan along the Lochwinnoch Road, Horton Township, brilliant yellow trefoil dominates a rejuvenated pasture two years after a frost seeding. The trefoil together with the bright blue sky and the red barn lend a vivid splash of colour to the countryside.

In 1998 Harvey and Jenny Crozier were 97 and 95 years of age, respectively. Married since 1933, they are one of Renfrew's oldest couples. Jenny explains, "We've been together just 65 years because, you see, we wedded late in life, when we were in our early 30's." Harvey adds, "We're lost if one's away."

The Irish, Germans, and Polish came to the highlands along the Opeongo Road to Grattan, Griffith, Sebastopol, and Brudenell townships. The settlers stoically picked rocks and dragged them to the edge of newly cleared fields, creating stone fences that still stand, visible reminders of their great effort.

On a sunny, winter day Sheila Keough pauses in the fresh powder snow along a ridge at Calabogie Peaks to enjoy the panoramic vista. The frozen expanse of Calabogie Lake is actually a widening of the Madawaska River, the water level being controlled by a dam in the village of Calabogie.

Through the years, a visit to Lynch's General Store at McDougall on County Road 5 was a treat not to be missed for a bit of news, gossip, and the chance to buy interesting and useful items. Leaving the store one day we saw Fluff, the neighbour's cat, sitting on the peeling picket fence by the red barn.

Pat and Zena Lynch and son, Martin, in front of Lynch's General Store one nippy November day in 1992. The store was built of sturdy logs by Peter Ferguson in 1889 on the Renfrew-Douglas road. In 1923 Zena's father, Joseph LaFleur, purchased the business, which remains in the family today.

Looking down Raglan Street from atop the O'Brien Building toward the Pinnacle. Until the mid-1850s Renfrew's commercial centre was predictably called Main Street. The street was renamed in honour of Fitzroy James Raglan, the British field marshal who commanded the British troops in the Crimean War.

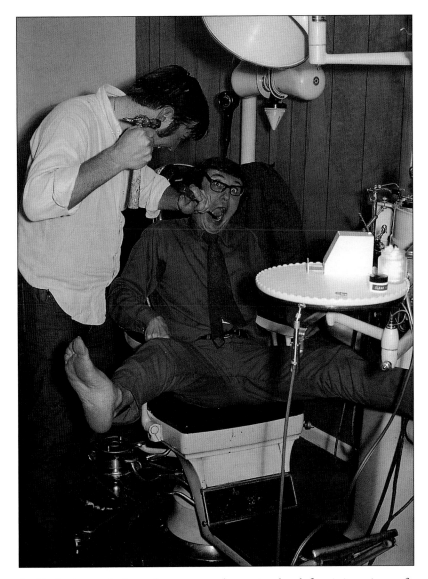

Jackie Ledger calmly and courageously awaits the deft ministrations of the young, new dentist in town, Dr. George Rouble, May 1970.

Upper: Undaunted by early snow, Jane Donnelly cycles along Harry Street.
Lower: This cornice, built c.1896, is above the Opeongo Bowling Lanes.

Mary Keough, with her red umbrella, adds a cheery note to a sodden day as she crosses Renfrew's historic swinging bridge over the Bonnechere River. Constructed in 1895 of spring coil wire decked with rough planking and no handrails, the 400-foot long bridge has since been made much safer.

While bicycling to Odd Fellows Park one spring morning in 1993 dozens of showy balloons attracted our attention. The balloons from the wedding reception of Candy and Sean Enright enliven the Reid home at 283 Renfrew Avenue East, where Shelly Reid stands with Katie and Quinn Guyea.

A solitary hawthorn tree stands proud in a meadow enhanced, from an aesthetic point of view, with colourful spikes of Blue-weed and a sprinkling of Black-eyed Susan and Queen Anne's Lace, a scene to be enjoyed in the rough of the century farm at Dragon Fly Golf Links southwest of town.

The combination of lines and patterns formed by the octopus-like splay of conveyor belts together with the conical piles of sorted stone at Nesbitt Aggregates was quite photogenic this sunny day. "The best little gravel pit in the Valley" has been operating since 1966 in Horton Township.

At freeze-up, the first light snowfall dusts the banks of Smith's Creek as it wends its way towards town past the red-roofed barn on the bend. This barn, now serving as a warehouse, was once a stable for the racehorses of Tom Barnet Sr. and Jr. and was used in the 1960s by the Renfrew Pony Club.

With a kindly smile and a twinkle in her eye Ethel Kobus, 85, credits her good health to daily walks and her enjoyment of skating and bowling.

Jack Collins, whose warm greeting was for years a fixture at Fraser's Clothes Shop, has likely outfitted more hunters than anyone else in the Valley.

This grand brick house with stone quoins and window trim is located on Renfrew Avenue East at Lynn Street. Believed built for 19th-century Renfrew businessman Peter Stewart, the dwelling was later home to Alexander Baird and his wife, Nan, a Stewart, and until the mid-1980s their daughter, Helen.

The congregation of the Renfrew Baptist Church was formed in 1882 and built this fine church of brick and stone in 1885. The building was among the first in town to have electric lights, thanks to A. A. Wright, owner of Renfrew's original generating plant and a staunch supporter of the Baptist faith.

The golden glow of evening settles on the placid waters of the Bonnechere River as it meanders through the rich farm country near Cotieville. Early French fur-traders and lumbermen named the river "Bonnechère," meaning good and dear, a description befitting much of the river's gentle character.

Upper: During the Winter Carnival, youngsters enjoy a game of shinny on the frozen Bonnechere River in the vicinity of Rainbow Crescent.

Lower Left: The classic prow of a wooden boat amid lilies on Hurd's Lake.
Lower Right: Bull-head waterlilies flourish in streams, lakes, and ponds.

Controversy swirls over the origin of the Cadieux home on Arnprior Ave. This sturdy log house, now covered with board and batten, was dragged on skids by teams of horses either from Thompson Hill in 1875 or, in order to make way for the O.A. & P.S. Railway (later the C.N.R.), from Prince Street in 1893.

By the fairgrounds near the end of Coumbes Lane there once stood an old barn. On the same site today a charming, sun-dappled garden has been created. Here, Joan Hickey spends a lot of time nurturing her flower beds, this one brightly accented with yellow Goldenglow and orange Tiger lilies.

Douglas, the picturesque village on the banks of the Bonnechere at Third Chute, is seen here in the last fading light of a winter's day. The McAllisters were the first settlers to come to the area back in 1828. The new hamlet was well established by 1838, with lumbering as the main activity.

Upper: In 1969 the Church of The Assumption stood above the drowned village of Black Donald and the lake created by Mountain Chute Dam.
Lower: Snowmobilers from Oxford Mills check directions along the trail at Renfrew while on an outing from Kemptville to Pembroke and back.

How things change! This photo, taken in 1970, includes Harold Mayhew standing beside his home southwest of Renfrew on Hwy 132. Beneath the white stucco is the original log house built around 1870. Present owners Lila and Ross Peever rejuvenated this residence and have faced it with red brick.

In Admaston Township, round, golden bales of alfalfa lie in Ross Peever's field that is greening with new growth. This scene is typical of farmland along the Bonnechere River in July. In the distance, Murray Galbraith's farm, with the three silos, lies below the heavily wooded Pinnacle Ridge.

Autumn paints the landscape in the Precambrian hills southwest of Eganville in Sebastopol Township. St. John's Lutheran Church, built in 1890 with its steeple added some 20 years later, stands beside the barely visible Opeongo Road. The island-dotted waters of Lake Clear add beauty to the scene.

On the east side of the Valley the home of Bill and Jean Winters overlooks the Ottawa River, the Gatineau Hills, and St. James Catholic Church in the village of Portage-du-Fort, Quebec. The Winters' home was built by David Price in the 1880s of massive ash logs up to two feet in diameter.

On one of those bitterly cold evenings when snow squeaks underfoot, the moon rises full over the snug, rustic home built by Dan and Kathleen Donohue in 1975 of logs reclaimed from three derelict buildings. This house, at Ferguslea, overlooks the famous, old colonization road, the Opeongo Line.

A hearty ho-ho-ho from jolly Saint Nick, Lions Club member Rob Lanyon, as he merrily greets young and old during the 1992 Santa Claus Parade.

Upper: The St. Joseph's High School Christmas float in the 1992 parade.
Lower: The Post Office Building viewed from Renfrew Avenue West.

Jack Nolan of Shamrock, file in hand, critically eyes the teeth of a crosscut saw. Renowned for his champion workhorses, Jack is also known for the heated discussions he can have with the likes of Mike Kelly and others regarding the fine art of sharpening saws, correcting the bite, and such.

In the 1800s the stately White pine drew lumbermen deeper into the Ottawa Valley, leading to the development of Renfrew, Eganville, Douglas, and other settlements. These colourful chainsaws, old and new, are a reminder that even today many people, at least part-time, continue to work the bush.

At top right is the major junction of Raglan, Coumbes, and Hall streets. Hall runs diagonally down to the left, intersecting Plaunt, Lynn, Barr, and Dominion streets. Coumbes Street, with Coumbes Lane branching off, passes between the Queen Elizabeth Public School and the fairgrounds.

Upper: A piano-box buggy in front of the old barns at the fairgrounds.
Lower: Colourful Shriners with their invisible dogs, clowning about.

The vivid berries of a Mountain ash and a touch of snow brighten this image of the Library building and Firehall tower on Railway Street.

Seated on his steam-powered buggy, mechanically inclined Ken Barber says, "If you don't know what you're doing, it will blast you to the moon."

Minni, the chestnut mule, looks out her trailer window after taking part in the Lumber Baron Parade with her owners, the Sadlers of Pakenham.

From Second Chute at Renfrew to First Chute just above the River Road at Castleford, the Bonnechere River is confined by high, often rocky banks. In this scene, east of Hwy 417 mist rises from the river, which is flowing out of sight in the wooded valley between the meadow and the sun.

Smith's Creek, which once powered several mills, including those of John Smith, flows through a tangled maze of standing and fallen Black willows.

A covey of doves gleans warmth atop the elevator head of the old flour mill and granary previously belonging to Ottawa Valley Grain Products.

Marjorie and Earl Lindsay relax on the lovely, expansive lawn of their home at 321 Albert Street North. The ivy-covered carriage house, with its double doors and loft above, was originally a barn built about 1880 when the main house was completed for businessman and magistrate George McDonald.

In 1883 Allan John Lindsay engaged a relative, George Macklem, to erect a novel eight-sided barn with hay storage above and stalls for cattle and sheep below. The "Round Barn" along Lochwinnoch Road in Horton Township has since become a landmark and is one of only two such barns in Ontario.

Even more interesting than the exterior of the Round Barn is the interior, particularly the roof structure. Rather rickety ladders lead up to the octagonal apex where spruce rafters, and the odd ash member, join to complete the geometric pattern designed and constructed so perfectly over a century ago.

In Springtown the Catholic Church of St. Gabriel overlooks the peaceful beauty of the Madawaska River. Back in 1854, when the church was built, Springtown was a bustling community, especially in spring when the river valley rang with the shouts of log drivers and the brawls of shantymen.

The pastoral countryside near Ferguslea in Admaston Township is crisscrossed by century-old cedar rail fences. Hand-split and stacked by the same hard-working settlers who made the rock piles, many of these fences are slowly being encroached upon by second- and third-generation growth.

Beryl Foley "just loves" the flowers outside her door at 91 Lisgar Avenue West. The five-unit row housing was built around 1918 by Tom Low to provide homes for employees working across the street at Low's Renfrew Electric Manufacturing Company, now the site of Our Lady of Fatima Catholic Church.

One cold, windless day, light snow gently settled on the berry clusters clinging to the gaunt, grey limbs of this Mountain ash. The colourful berries and the red-brick chimney were graphically juxtaposed against the simple white stucco wall and snow-covered roof of 72 Renfrew Avenue West.

After four years of good crop, the field had "run out." One November day Manfred Thomssen took a short break from turning the soil in preparation for planting alfalfa next spring. Manfred didn't mind a little teasing about the wobble at the end of his section, as seen from the South McNaughton Line.

Upper: Cream-coloured Charolais, by reputation one of the best beef cattle breeds, quietly graze a high pasture in scenic Matawatchan Township.
Lower: Renfrew's C.N.R. line is history and in 1984 the tracks were removed. The right-of-way has since become an enjoyable recreation trail.

The sawmill at Balaclava stands forlorn and silent beside the babbling waters of Constan Creek. Through the latter 1800s and into the mid-1900s, outflow from the dam, just visible upstream, powered the machinery in the mill to saw and plane lumber, to produce shingles, and even to make hash for pigs.

This old trail leads to the abandoned settlement of Newfoundout in the Opeongo Hills. When Irish homesteaders such as the O'Briens, Donohues, and Parkers came to this stony country, which was "new" and they had "found it out," there were "so many rocks there was hardly room for a potato hill."

Each February as the days lengthen and sun is a little stronger, Renfrew celebrates at the Winter Carnival. Next to a warming fire on the bank of the Bonnechere, members of the Gauthier clan, Darrel, Todd, and Bonnie with sons Joshua and Tyler, show their catch following the Pike Fishing Derby.

In simpler times, grades one through eight took their lessons in the one-room, red-brick school house in Brougham Township at the edge of Dacre. This traditional school was built in 1917, decommissioned in 1967, and was used thereafter as a township office until, unfortunately, it burned about 1979.

Bass-man "Baley" welcomes all comers to the Valley Bluegrass Festival, an annual event held at Bob and Julie Johnston's farm in Horton Township.

Matthew Felhaber of Eganville watches his mom, Polly, participate in the women's crosscut saw event at the Lumberjack Show in the fairgrounds.

Henry Moore's bales lie scattered about a field along old Hwy 17 east of town. Only a century ago, hay was coiled by hand. Then came the horse-drawn binder producing sheaves that were hand-stooked. Next came the familiar square bales, which are themselves being supplanted by these large, round bales.

Below the "mountain" on the Ferguson Lake Road stands the old Paddy McNulty homestead, built in 1850 of massive White pine logs. Proud owners Wilf and Janet O'Brien have done much to restore the property. Conveniently located left of the house is the former summer kitchen, now a woodshed.

At the foot of the Pinnacle stands the cheerful home of Jean Elliott, which has belonged to her family since 1933. The house, with its gingerbread trim and ornate quoins and windows, was built around 1876 by Joshua Murphy, a prosperous entrepreneur whose brick buildings grace downtown Renfrew.

Above: Kelly Anglin takes her little niece Madison Reitz trick-or-treating.
Lower Right: A Sugar maple in full blaze, a common and glorious fall sight.

Upper: The Jamieson Lime Kilns, which still stand beside Lime Kiln Road, produced quality lime for mortar and gold refining from 1865 to 1950.

Snow swirls about the bell tower, roof, and Celtic cross of St. Paul's Anglican Church, an elegant structure built in 1900 and styled after an English cathedral. In the chancel are a few pews bearing cinder burns. These pews were all that was salvaged from the fire that destroyed the previous church.

The workers at Campbell's sawmill in Ferguslea halt their efforts momentarily for the camera. Tim Megrath is front centre, Andy Byers is at the left and Ross Campbell is furthest away. This fully operational, diesel-powered sawmill processes an impressive 1/2 million board feet of pine and poplar each year.

Skilled lumbermen Donald Campbell and his son Ross stand by their 48" circular head saw, with three other circular blades stored nearby on the wall behind them. Donald, an energetic octogenarian, built the mill between 1957 and 1960 as time and money permitted. Ross now operates the mill.

The fury and sound of tumbling water were music to the ears of Francis Hincks, John Lorn McDougall, and other visionaries of the 1850s. The Bonnechere River at Second Chute powered the new mills and instilled vitality into the fledgling community that was developing around this site.

Upper: Mike Rouble's barn, photographed in 1985, stands no more along Hwy 60. An April storm lifted the roof and the top three rounds of logs.

Lower Left: The wood of the lovely White ash makes hard, resilient handles.
Lower Right: Staghorn sumach displays foliage reminiscent of the tropics.

The solemnity of Remembrance Day, November 11th, is symbolized by poppies, wreaths, and crosses. Members of the community gather about the cenotaph at Low Square in front of the town hall to commemorate those local men and women who went away to war and made the supreme sacrifice.

Upper Left: Paul Allen, Sgt.-at-Arms, smartly leads the Legionnaires.
Upper Right: A speeder patrolling the C.P.R. line passes by Jennet Street.

Lower: Gerald Keough is an ardent and active flyer in his 80's. Also known as the town's great walker, Gerry covers six miles daily, regardless of weather.

Betty and Haley Flower's lovely country home faces onto Byers Road near Hurd's Lake. The front door leads into what was once Admaston S.S. #1 school, built about 1890. To create the extension to the right, Betty and Haley relocated the 150-year-old Ferguslea blacksmith shop of Maurice Culhane.

Steam is one of Dr. Bill Burwell's passions in life. William Miller had told him of some old machinery rotting in his barn. This proved to be a treasure for Bill and a few friends, who restored the antiquated steam-powered dragsaw to full operation. "Bill really loves his toys," says his wife, Diane.

In mid-July Justin Brenner unintentionally creates abstract art on a field just off Hwy 417 near the Bonnechere River where he was raking hay into windrows. The rake fluffs up the hay, enabling it to air-dry prior to baling. In this hot weather the round baler followed a couple of hours later.

We made two photographs of the Gilchrist barn on Holmes Road southwest of town. One picture *(see back cover)* features the entire barn with the gate and pathway. The second image, seen here, focusses on a portion of the barn's silo, siding, and roof. Artistically, this simpler composition appeals to us.

There is no more glorious time in the Valley than those Indian summer days of early October when the ash, oak, and maple turn colour. There is no more beautiful an area to experience autumn than up in the rolling, rocky country west of Renfrew, where heritage and nature blend so harmoniously.

Upper: The lively First Chute of the Bonnechere River near Castleford.
Lower Left: Ralph Eady's fieldstone house, built in 1845 on the River Road.

Lower Right: The Holy Well, blessed in 1870, runneth over. Actually, Constan Creek floods the well and the priests' graves at Mt. St. Patrick.

Those in the know claim that rocks are among the most reliable crop in parts of the Valley. "You don't have to plant them and they come back every year." In a recently cultivated field just off the Burnstown Road at Smith's Creek, Jack Wallace, with the fork, interrupted his stone picking-operation to chat.

One fine Sunday morning Jack Wallace and Tom Dedo were chewing a quid down by the barn while discussing the rights and wrongs of the world. Tom (who Jack says is just crawling over 75 years) is rather opinionated. "If I got up in a pulpit, I'd say it like it is. Next week they'd have to get a larger church."

In McNab Township on the north side of Burnstown, the Campbell family in 1844 built this home of huge White pine logs squared, some to 14" x 24", with the broad axe. The pioneer home remained in the family for the next 150 years until Catherine Campbell McIntyre passed away in 1994.

The warmer days of March break winter's grip on Eastwood Falls where Locha Creek tumbles into a gorge below Brae-Loch Road, Horton Township. Today at this lovely wild spot there is little sign of past industry: the brick and tile works above the falls, the grist mill and carpet factory below.

In a 1970 scene that kindles nostalgic memories, bachelor Mike Kelly drives his team hitched to a set of sloops along English Road in Admaston Township. Lightning, the black at left, is a Percheron. Sandy, the chestnut, is a Belgian. Mike was shortly thereafter "taken" by Dianne Caldwell.

The lovely Catholic Church of Saint Patrick in the picturesque hamlet of Mount St. Patrick was constructed as a frame building in 1869 under the direction of tireless missionary Father John McNulty. In 1929 the church was renovated and faced with stone from Joe English's quarry nearby.

For a nominal five shillings and the promise to build a stone grist mill, John Lorn McDougall purchased a quarter acre of land adjacent to Second Chute from Francis Hincks in 1855. The well-constructed building is seen here a century and a half later from across the Renfrew Hydro headpond.

A fresh, spring day in McConnell Park looking across Smith's Creek to the pathway snaking up the hill toward Vimy Blvd. on Tiger Island.

Upper: The charming Klinowski home at 95 Quarry Avenue, built in 1890.
Lower: Fairground barns built after the 1904 fire and demolished in 1991.

Upper: Horses graze at the old Hanniman farm on the Ferguslea Road.
Lower: Detail of doors, lintel, chinking, and toggles supporting the logs.

Lower Right: Detail of the hand-hewn, dove-tailed corner of 38 Lochiel Street, Wally and Jackie Bigford's log house that was built in 1870.

In a few months the sap will flow in the sugar bush on the rise behind Harold Nolan's barn along the Burnstown Road. This large "bank" barn, built around 1932 for Dr. James Wallace, is set into the hillside, thus allowing easy access to the hay storage above. In winter, cattle are kept in the stalls below.

The Bonnechere River snakes through town and is crossed just above Second Chute by Bridge Street. Below the bridge is Renfrew Hydro's headpond, dam, and power plant. Across the river is the historic McDougall Mill, while just a short distance downstream is the famous swinging bridge.

Local lakes, streams, ponds, and the Bonnechere River have spawned their share of tall fish tales and, from time to time, witnessed a little political intrigue. Rub a dub dub, two mayors in a tub! Here, Howie Haramis receives some sage advice from Audrey Green on the finer points of unhooking a garpike.

In Renfrew no scene is better recognized or appreciated than the delightful view downstream from the west end of the bridge over the Bonnechere. The river, tumbling and dancing over the rapids, leads the eye to the picturesque McDougall Mill Museum on the bend — an artist's inspiration.

On a balmy spring day our daughter, Rebekka Dawn, enjoys the slide, the swings, and the carpet of jaunty dandelions at Odd Fellows Park. Renfrew is blessed with many public green spaces thanks to good planning by numerous residents spanning the years back to Xavier Plaunt and Francis Hincks.

Smith's Creek, after flowing 6.5 miles from Hurd's Lake, empties into the Bonnechere through the finely cut stone culvert beneath the C.P.R. tracks. At the mouth of the creek, George Foster fishes for pike and pickerel. A few casts later he gave up when a Snapping turtle went after his lure.

The mid-July day had been hot and humid, the temperature pushing 100°F/38°C. In the farm country west of Cotieville, beyond the line of trees growing along the Bonnechere River, clouds began to gather in the late afternoon. The setting sun lights the cloud-filled sky. Perhaps rain will come in the night.

PHOTO: DAVID BARKER

PAT & ROSEMARIE KEOUGH are photographers and authors of some of the best-selling art books ever produced in Canada. Their first publication, *The Ottawa Valley Portfolio,* was followed by *The Nahanni Portfolio* and *The Niagara Escarpment: A Portfolio.* A second series of quality Keough books includes *Beautiful Arnprior, Wild and Beautiful Sable Island,* and, now, *The Beauty of Renfrew and Area.* Photographs by Rosemarie and Pat have been published in numerous books and magazines in North America and Europe. Currently their images appear as part of an international art exhibition and companion book featuring Alaska's Copper River Delta. In addition to their publishing ventures, the Keoughs have appeared on numerous television shows, the most notable being the award-winning *Nahanni and Rebekka Dawn.*

Renfrew was Pat's home town. His parents, Gerald and Mary Keough, continue to live on Coumbes Lane, while family members are scattered throughout the Ottawa Valley. Pat and Rosemarie now live in the Gulf Islands of British Columbia. Between world travels they return whenever possible to the Valley with their children, Rebekka Dawn and Glen.

The Keoughs extend a very sincere note of thanks to family and friends who have lent assistance, especially to Bob & Birgit Bateman, Carol Bennett, David Bishop, Jeffrey Collins, Kathleen & Dan Donohue, Alex & Hans Fischer, Larry Frank, Jack & Ruth Grant, Audrey Green, Howard & Wayne Haramis, Mike & Dianne Kelly, Gerald & Mary Keough, Rev. Dr. Martin Kreplin, Otto & Ingrid Lachmund, Earl & Marjorie Lindsay, Jean Lynch, Michael Mayzel, Uwe Mummenhoff, Margaret & Anthony Pocket, Peter Scarth, Wilf Simpson, Alex Tilley, Isabel Wallace, the Renfrew Public Library, and the National Archives of Canada at Renfrew.

The Renfrew and Area Seniors' Home Support — its staff, directors, and volunteers — and the **Fundraising Committee** deserve special recognition for their worthy efforts. Although it is not possible to name everyone, appreciation is extended to Chris Cobus, Maureen MacDonald, Angie Lepine, Earl Bennett, Judy Campbell, Jack & Shirley Collins, Rudy Cooper, Lawrence Gallagher, Joe Gauthier, Jean Henderson, Lewis MacDonald, Harry Mayhew, Joan Reid, Isobel Richmond, Doug Rouble, Carol Ann Simson, Angela Vice, and Burt Virgin.

All proceeds from this book, *The Beauty of Renfrew and Area,* benefit the Renfrew and Area Seniors' Home Support. The success of this fundraising effort has been greatly assisted by the involvement of *The Renfrew Mercury.* The Keoughs and The Renfrew and Area Seniors' Home Support wish to acknowledge and express their true appreciation to Fred Runge, Derek Walter, Lucy Hass, and the rest of the staff at this fine newspaper.

THE BEAUTY OF RENFREW AND AREA

Photography, Research, Writing, Design & Publishing	Pat & Rosemarie Keough Nahanni Productions Inc.
Editing	Heather Lang-Runtz
Proofreading	Mary Keough
History Advisor	Marjorie Lindsay
Colour Separation, Printing & Binding	Friesens Corporation Manitoba, Canada